Coaches

by Katie Bagley

Consultant:
Robert Ferraro
Executive Director
National High School Coaches Association

Bridgestone Books
an imprint of Capstone Press
Mankato, Minnesota

Bridgestone Books are published by Capstone Press
151 Good Counsel Drive, P.O. Box 669, Mankato, Minnesota 56002
http://www.capstone-press.com

Library of Congress Cataloging-in-Publication Data
Bagley, Katie.
    Coaches/by Katie Bagley.
    p. cm.—(Community helpers)
    Includes bibliographical references and index.
    ISBN 0-7368-0807-8
    1. Coaches (Athletics)—Juvenile literature. 2. Coaching (Athletics)—Vocational
guidance—Juvenile literature. [1. Coaches (Athletics) 2. Coaching (Athletics) 3. Occupations.]
I. Title. II. Community helpers (Mankato, Minn.)
GV711 .B25 2001
796' .07'7—dc21
                                                                                00-009700

Summary: A simple introduction to the work coaches do, tools they use, skills they need,
    and their importance to the communities they serve.

Editorial Credits
Sarah Lynn Schuette, editor; Karen Risch, product planning editor; Heather Kindseth,
    cover designer; Heidi Schoof, photo researcher

Photo Credits
Bill and Debbie Adamson, 12
GeoIMAGERY/The PhotoNews/Clark Brooks, 10
James L. Shaffer, 6, 8, 14, 16, 20
Jim Cummins/FPG International LLC, cover
Jim West/Impact Visuals, 4
Unicorn Stock Photos/Mark Romesser, 18

1 2 3 4 5 6 06 05 04 03 02 01

Table of Contents

Coaches

Coaches are people who teach and train athletes to play sports. They show athletes how to play by the rules. Coaches help team members learn how to work together.

athlete

someone who is trained to play a sport

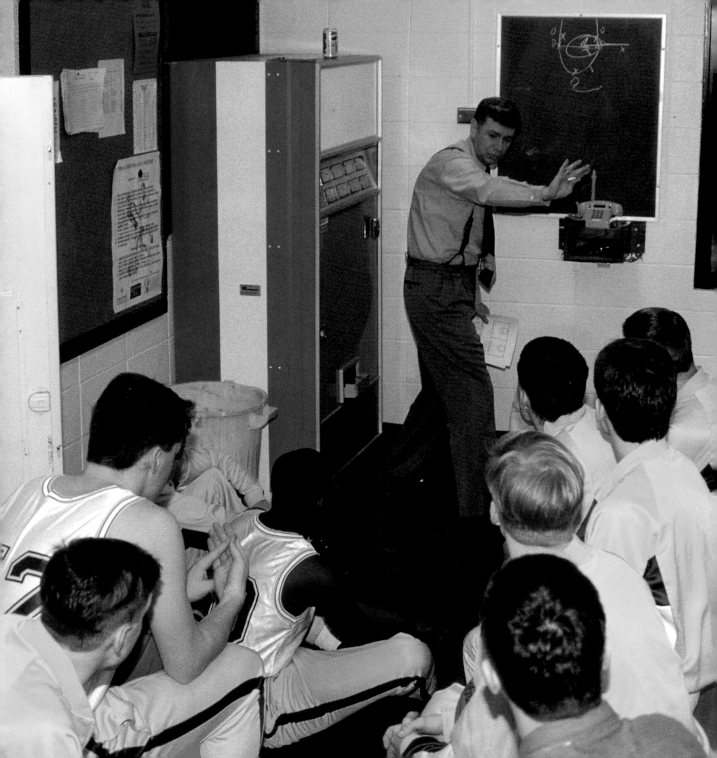

What Coaches Do

Coaches watch athletes practice. They tell athletes and teams how to improve their skills. Coaches make game plans. They also decide what positions players will play.

game plan
drawings or directions for making certain plays during a game; good game plans help teams play well.

Different Kinds of Coaches

Head coaches train a whole team. Assistant coaches help head coaches make game plans. Volunteer coaches often coach community teams. They do not get paid for their work. Other coaches work for professional teams.

professional team

a group of players who are paid to play a sport

Where Coaches Work

Many coaches work in grade schools, middle schools, high schools, and colleges. They coach athletes on playing fields, in gyms, and on courts. They may coach sporting events indoors or outdoors.

college
a place where people study after high school

Some Coaches Are Teachers

Some coaches who work in schools also are teachers. They teach many subjects in classrooms. Coaches often lead gym classes or teach health classes.

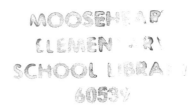

Tools Coaches Use

Coaches speak into megaphones to help athletes hear them. They blow whistles to get players' attention. Coaches use stopwatches to time races. They also use first aid kits to help athletes who get hurt.

megaphone

a tool shaped like a cone that makes a person's voice sound louder

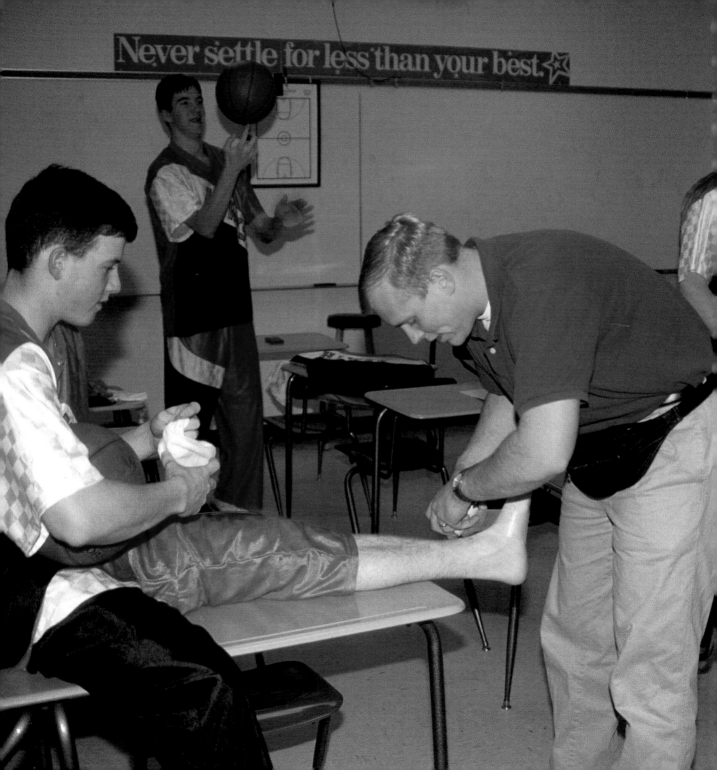

Never settle for less than your best.

Coaches and School

Many coaches play on teams to learn their sport. People who want to be coaches sometimes go to college. They take classes to learn about coaching and first aid. Coaches also learn how to treat and prevent injuries.

injury
damage or harm
to the body

People Who Help Coaches

Assistant coaches and volunteers help coaches teach skills. Parents encourage athletes and bring them to practice on time. Referees and umpires make sure players follow the rules of a sport. Athletic trainers help coaches treat injuries.

encourage

to give support; parents and coaches encourage athletes to do their best.

How Coaches Help Others

Coaches help people learn to work together. They encourage teams to play well. Coaches teach athletes to do their best at a sport. Coaches help athletes and spectators have fun.

spectator
someone who watches a sport or an event

Hands On: Coach a Game

Coaches teach people how to play sports. You can teach your friends how to play a game and play with them.

What You Need

Two teams with an equal number of players
One tennis ball for each player
Permanent marker
Beanbag
Open space to play

What You Do

1. Mark each ball with the marker to tell the balls apart. You also could use different colored tennis balls.
2. Decide which team will go first.
3. The coach throws the beanbag about 5 yards (4.6 meters) away.
4. The object of the game is to get the ball closest to the beanbag. Each player takes a turn and throws one ball at the beanbag.
5. The coach gives one point to the team that threw the ball closest to the beanbag. The coach throws the beanbag again.
6. The first team to get five points wins.

Words to Know

college (KOL-ij)—a place where students study after high school

first aid kit (FURST AID KIT)—a set of items such as bandages used to help sick or injured people

referee (ref-uh-REE)—someone who watches a sports match or game to make sure players follow the rules

stopwatch (STOP-watch)—a watch that can be started and stopped; coaches often use stopwatches to time races or other events.

umpire (UHM-pire)—an official who rules on plays in baseball, tennis, and other sports

volunteer (vol-uhn-TEER)—someone who does a job without getting paid

Read More

Bowman-Kruhm, Mary, and Claudine G. Wirths. *A Day in the Life of a Coach.* The Kids' Career Library. New York: PowerKids Press, 1997.

Dubois, Muriel L. *I Like Sports: What Can I Be?* Mankato, Minn.: Bridgestone Books, 2000.

Internet Sites

Get Fit! Don't Quit!
http://tqjunior.thinkquest.org/4139
Playing it Safe with Sports Safety for Kids
http://www.kidshealth.org/kid/watch/out/sport_safety.html
Sport! Science
http://www.exploratorium.edu/sports

Index